Persistent Prayer

Equipping the body of Christ to persist in prayer through a variety of prayer efforts in order to gain a position of authority over the enemy and fulfill the calling of the Lord Jesus in their lives.

by Clyde J Hodson

All rights reserved. No part of this book may be reproduced in any form without permission in writing from the author, except in the case of brief quotations em-bodied in critical articles or reviews.

All scripture quotations are taken from the Holy Bible: New International Version (NIV) or the New American Standard Bible (NASB).

Copyright © 2011 by Clyde Hodson

All rights reserved

ISBN-13: 978-1719013246

ISBN-10: 1719013241

I want to thank Jack Jackson and Larry Yandell for reading through this material and giving valuable input to its final product. A special thanks is in order to Beth Marshall for her encouragement and contribution to the editing of this booklet. I am grateful to my wife, Mary Lynne, and my daughters, Kara, Lindsay and Meagan for all the early mornings and evenings they allowed me to pray with others who were in need through various kinds of prayer efforts.

For more prayer resources please contact:

Clyde Hodson

PrayerMentor

PO Box 13856

Arlington, TX 76094

(682) 472-7378

clydehodson@prayermentor.org

www.prayermentor.org

Table of Contents

Introduction 7

    Persistent Prayer In The Early Church 7

    Persistent Asking, Seeking & Knocking 9

    Jesus Taught Persistent Prayer 12

    The Resistance of the Enemy 14

Prayer Efforts 19

    Daniel Prayer Effort 21

    Prayerful Disciple Making 23

    Jericho Prayer Effort 26

    On-Site Geographical Prayer 28

    Overseas Jericho Prayer Team 30

    Prayer Partners 32

    Prayer Walks 34

    Twenty-four Hour Fast 36

    Twenty-four Hour Silent Retreat 38

    Wilderness Prayer Effort 42

Appendix 47

    Encountering God Together 49

Notes 59

About the Author 61

Introduction

Persistent Prayer In The Early Church

The resources of heaven are available to the Christian leader who will persist in prayer and mobilize other members of the body of Christ to join him in a persistent work of prayer. Persistent prayer was the model of the early church. The early church continually devoted itself to prayer.

After Jesus instructs His followers to remain in Jerusalem, they all join together constantly in prayer. They pray and Matthias is added to the eleven apostles. (Acts 1:12-26)

For ten days they are together in one place and the Holy Spirit is poured out on the day of Pentecost. Peter declares the truth of what is happening and 3,000 are added to their number. (Acts 2:1-41)

The infant church devotes itself to the apostles' teaching, the fellowship, the breaking of bread and prayer; as a result the Lord adds to their number daily those who are being saved. (Acts 2:42-47)

While Peter and John are walking to a prayer gathering, a lame man is healed. Peter preaches the Gospel, many who hear the message believe and the number increases to five thousand men. (Acts 3:1-4:4)

After Peter and John are released from prison, the believers pray, and they are filled with the Spirit and speak the word of God boldly. (Acts 4:23-37)

The apostles appoint deacons to wait on tables so they can give themselves to prayer and the ministry of the word. As a result, the number of the disciples increases rapidly and a large number of priests become obedient to the faith. (Acts 6:1-7)

When the apostles arrive in Samaria, they pray for the new Samaritan believers that they might receive the Holy Spirit. Peter and John then place their hands on them and they receive the Holy Spirit. (Acts 8:14-17)

When the Lord reveals Himself to Saul on the road to Damascus, he is blinded for three days. As Saul is praying in Damascus, he sees Ananias in a vision. Ananias responds to God's call and goes to place his hands on Saul. Saul's sight is restored, he is filled with the Holy Spirit and he begins to preach in the synagogues. (Acts 9:9-22)

Peter prays and Tabitha is raised from the dead. (Acts 9:32-42)

One day, as Cornelius, a Roman Centurion, is praying, he has a vision of an angel. In obedience to the angel's words, he sends three men to find Peter. The following day Peter is praying, falls into a trance and has a vision that moves him to go to Cornelius' home. While he is speaking to Cornelius and his household, the Holy Spirit falls upon them and the gentiles receive Christ for the first time. (Acts 10:1-48)

After Peter is put in prison, the church prays earnestly for him and an angel appears to him. His chains fall off and an angel leads him out of the prison. (Acts 12:1-11)

In Antioch, five prophets and teachers pray and the Holy Spirit calls Barnabas and Saul to a new work. After more fasting and prayer, they place their hands on Barnabas and Saul and send them off on their first missionary journey. (Acts 13:1-5)

The early church devotes itself continually to prayer. It is obvious that prayer is a way of life for the followers of Christ. They pray in a variety of ways, at a variety of times, for a variety of reasons. These followers pray for 10 days, 3 days, all night prayer vigils, at regular times of the day, in times of need and for ministry opportunities. They pray in large and small groups, with leadership teams, with partners and as individuals. They pray at the temple, in upper rooms, in their homes, at sick beds and on roofs. When the body of Christ prays, the word of God spreads, the number of the disciples are added to the church, the Spirit is poured out, leadership is raised up, the lame and sick are healed, and signs and wonders are performed.

The purpose of this booklet is to equip the Body of Christ to pray persistently, calling on the goodness and justice of God for the resources of heaven to fulfill the will of the Lord Jesus and meet the needs of those who are hurting. So many Christian leaders, whether parents, small group leaders, Sunday school class teachers or pastors are not fulfilling the responsibility entrusted to them by God because they don't persist in prayer and are not mobilizing others to join them in a persistent work of prayer. The prayer efforts detailed in this book will hopefully guide you into fruitful times of prayer; times in which you will watch your Heavenly Father show His goodness and justice in answering your prayers.

Persistent Asking, Seeking & Knocking

Through the years, the Lord has taught me many lessons about persistence in prayer. Jesus taught His disciples to always pray and not give up praying. The very tense of the verbs He uses in exhorting His disciples to pray emphasizes persistence in prayer. As a young believer, I was mentored by a man of prayer, Dave Griener. Dave, who was my youth pastor, told me, "If I can do nothing else, I can pray." This thought would come to him in times of frustration and inadequacy in his ministry. Dave led a youth group in a small church. Every night Dave rose at 2 or 3 in the early morning hours to pray for the students within his ministry. Out of that small youth group, ten students, my wife and myself included, entered full time vocational Christian ministry. I began a life of prayer as a result of Dave's teaching and modeling of prayer.

As a young pastor, I found myself in a negative cycle of prayer. The cycle usually started whenever I became frustrated with ministry. Dave's words would ring in my ears, and I would withdraw from the busyness of ministry in those times and pray. I would draw near to the throne of grace in a fresh way. At first it was wonderful! Jesus was on the throne and I was filled with new hope in the love and power of God to minister to the lives of the students and adults He entrusted to me. Then a downward cycle would begin and I would see my hope waning after a few weeks. I found myself becoming resentful in four weeks, and I was downright bitter in eight weeks. My feeling was, "These people aren't changing!" Finally, at the end of the cycle, I would have to throw away my prayer list because it was a constant reminder of my failure. Three to four months later I would become frustrated with ministry again and Dave's words rang in my ears once again; "If I can do nothing else, I can pray." So I withdrew from the busyness of ministry and my prayer cycle would begin again. From drawing near to the Lord and finding new hope in the love and power of Christ, to growing resentful when I didn't see any change I wanted, and finally, to giving up because I was downright bitter. The cycle would run its course again and again. Although there were many moments of watching the Lord answer prayer, this disappointing cycle repeated itself two to three times a year for twelve years.

In 1984, I was frustrated once again. I was humbled and ready to learn from the Lord. The Lord showed me His kindness when He led me to read, Prayer: Key To Revival, by Dr. Paul Cho. In his book, Dr. Cho teaches that prayer is more than praying through lists. The Lord gave me three key concepts during that time:

1. Prayer is seeking intimacy with the Lord Jesus.
2. Prayer is listening to the Holy Spirit.[1]
3. Prayer is asking, seeking and knocking.

Now, when my prayers go unanswered and I am tempted to resent those on my prayer list, I seek the face of the Lord Jesus. I begin listening. The Holy Spirit shows me what Jesus is doing and He gives me new insights into how to pray. There is a relationship between asking, seeking and knocking in prayer.[2] I find myself seeking intimacy with the Lord Jesus when I begin to feel emotions of resentment. The Spirit of God gives me new insights into how to pray, as I wait and listen. The negative cycle of defeat in prayer is broken. I begin experiencing answers to prayer more regularly, as the Spirit leads me to pray persistently. Through the years, the Lord has taught me that:

1. **Asking** - is making requests of the Father for the things we need.

2. **Seeking** - is pursuing oneness/intimacy with Jesus and the Father, listening for what God is saying and doing.

3. **Knocking** - is interceding for the transformation of a life, a family, a church, a city or a nation.

There is a relationship between all three of these kinds of prayer that ebbs and flows from one to the other as the Spirit leads. In 2 Corinthians 12:8, Paul says that, "...three times he pleaded with the Lord," to take away a thorn in the flesh. This is the Apostle Paul writing these words while in Ephesus. God did extraordinary miracles through Paul in Ephesus, so that even handkerchiefs and aprons that had touched him were taken to the sick, and they were cured and the evil spirits left them. And yet, God did not remove Paul's thorn in the flesh from him. Paul prayed three times. He may have pleaded with God three times in one season of prayer or in three separate seasons of prayer. We don't know how long of a period he prayed. It could have been for one hour or one day or seven days or even forty days. The Scriptures don't make it clear. I want to suggest Paul asked the Father to heal him during a season of prayer. When he didn't get healed, he sought the Lord's face to understand what He was doing. Not receiving any new insight, the Apostle entered into a second season of prayer. When there was no answer to his pleading with God, Paul sought the face of the Lord in a new way to hear what He was doing. Hearing no word from the Father, Paul entered into a third season of petition for his own healing. When that season of prayer was over, the Apostle sought the Lord's face for a third time. It was at that time the Lord spoke to him and said, "My grace is sufficient for you, for My power is made perfect in weakness." In this example of Paul, we observe the relationship between the three natures of prayer in persistent asking, seeking, and knocking.

Jesus Taught Persistent Prayer

I find that many pastors and Christian leaders in America do not engage in prayer. They are people of action by the very nature of their leadership roles. They have a hard time being still and waiting on the Lord. The notion of giving up control and waiting on God is too hard to handle. Because they do not persist in prayer, they do not see answered prayer. As a result, they don't really believe that prayer works. They will never admit unbelief, but their prayerlessness and the absence of leadership in prayer with their followers indicates it. As a result, many American Christians have no real practice of prayer and their lives are filled with the busyness of life and ministry. Our lives reflect the teachings of Jesus concerning the end times, when He said, "Just as it was in the days of Noah, so also will it be in the days of the Son of Man. People were eating, drinking, marrying and being given in marriage up to the day Noah entered the ark. Then the flood came and destroyed them all. It was the same in the days of Lot. People were eating and drinking, buying and selling, planting and building. But the day Lot left Sodom, fire and sulfur rained down from heaven and destroyed them all." Luke 17:26-29

We are busy with life and ministry. We believe in the power of God. We express faith in Him as we pray for those who are in need. But we don't see our prayers being answered because we don't persist in prayer, so we become consumed with the business of life. In raising our families, we are overwhelmed with homework, practices, lessons, games, etc. and we don't have time to intercede for the needs of others. The forty-hour work week has stretched to fifty and sixty hours and we just don't think we have time to pray. As a result, we have become indifferent to those who struggle with physical or emotional illness. We have accepted family conflict and divorce as common place. We have settled for the American way of life and adopted a Christianity shaped by the culture of the day. We don't see the supernatural hand of God at work in our lives because we don't persist in prayer.

There are two parables of persistence in prayer that Jesus taught His disciples. The first is the parable of the persistent neighbor in Luke 11. The second is the parable of the persistent widow in Luke 18. In the former, Jesus paints a portrait of a desperate man needing bread and teaches the truth of a persistent pursuit of the goodness of God. In the latter, Jesus gives a picture of a desperate widow in need of justice and teaches the truth of a persistent pursuit of the justice of God. In both examples, Jesus emphasizes the importance of persistence in prayer.

Jesus taught the first parable in response to the disciple's request for Him to teach them about prayer. This is the only time throughout Jesus' ministry it is recorded that the disciples asked Him to teach them anything. Many Bible teachers have taught that their request was a noble one. But I don't think so. I believe Jesus' disciples were frustrated with Him. As they asked Jesus to teach them about prayer, they compared Him to John the Baptist, "Lord, teach us to pray, just as John taught his disciples." These men felt John had given his disciples the secrets to answered prayer, but Jesus was holding out on them. They had watched Jesus pray and seen the supernatural answers to His prayers. They were desperate to learn Jesus' secret to answered prayer. Jesus' response was remarkable. He taught them the same truths about prayer He had taught in the past in the Sermon on the Mount. However, this time He adds a little story about a man who has a friend come to visit after a long journey. When he goes to the kitchen cupboards, he finds them bare. He has no food to set before his friend to refresh him after traveling so far. He is desperate. So he goes to his neighbor and asks for food to give to his friend. It is late at night and his neighbor has locked the house up and gone to bed. He doesn't want to help him. But because of his persistence the neighbor finally relents and gives him what he needs. Jesus is not comparing the neighbor with God in this parable. The point Jesus is making in this parable is that because the man is desperate, having no resources, he persistently seeks someone who does.

Jesus then repeats His previous teaching of persistent asking, persistent seeking and persistent knocking. Again, He gives the picture of a father giving good gifts to his children. As we have people come to us who are in need and we go to our cupboards and find them bare, we need to remember that we have a Heavenly Father who is good. He has all the resources we need and He desires to give us good gifts, as we persistently ask Him for them. The key is that we are persistent in the asking, seeking and knocking.

The second parable Jesus taught on persistence in prayer is the story of the persistent widow. He told them this parable to show His followers that they should always pray and not to give up praying. In this parable, there is a widow who goes to a judge who neither fears God nor man, seeking justice from her adversary. The judge couldn't be bothered with her. But, because of her desperation and persistence, he relents and gives her justice. Jesus is not comparing this unjust judge to God; rather He is making a contrast between the two. As opposed to the unjust judge, God is just. The unjust judge couldn't be bothered, but God will bring justice to those who cry out to Him day and night. God will do it quickly. The key to finding justice is persistence in prayer. Jesus is emphasizing the importance of a dogged, relentless pursuit of someone in authority who can bring justice to a situation. That someone is our just God.

The Resistance of the Enemy

Why persistence in prayer? It is interesting that Jesus never explains why we are to persist in prayer. He just emphasizes persistence repeatedly. I want to suggest the reason for persistence in prayer is the spiritual battle that is taking place in the heavenly places. The Word of God describes an enemy and a spiritual conflict:

- The devil comes to rob, kill and destroy. (John 10:10)
- There are demonic strongholds, arguments and pretensions, which set themselves up against the knowledge of God. (II Cor. 10:4,5)
- We don't wrestle against flesh and blood but against rulers, against the authorities, against the powers of this dark world

and against the spiritual forces of evil in the heavenly realms. (Ephesians 6:12)

As we persist in prayer, we are warring with the powers of darkness. There are doors that only the Lord Jesus can open and close. Through persistent knocking, Jesus will open them. There is bondage in people's lives that only persistent prayer will release. It is through persistent asking, seeking and knocking that we will overcome the works of the devil.

The Old Testament illustrates the need for persistent prayer when warring with the powers of darkness. Daniel had a visitation from an angel after a 21 day fast that gives insight into the spiritual conflict that takes place in the heavenly realms as we pray.

Daniel receives a vision from God, but he doesn't understand it, so he humbles himself before God and begins to fast on the day he first received the vision. On the twenty-first day, the angel tells Daniel that he was sent to give him the interpretation of the vision the very day he started fasting, twenty-one days prior. But another angel, an enemy of God, hindered him from coming to Daniel, and Michael, the angel of Israel, assisted him in the battle so that he could finally come to Daniel. Through the intercession of Daniel's prayer and fasting, the angel was able to overcome the dark angel and give the interpretation of the vision to Daniel. How many times do we pray and God sends His angels to bring the answer? However, we stop praying and the powers of darkness overcome in the heavenly conflict. As a result, we never receive the answer to our intercession. We are to persist in prayer because there is a spiritual battle in the heavenly places and the powers of darkness want to rob us of God's blessing.

The challenge for the American Christian today is to break away from the busyness of life and enter into this spiritual battle through persistent prayer. Jesus' final question after He tells the parable of the persistent widow is very convicting. Jesus asks, "However, when the Son of Man comes, will He find faith on the earth?" Why does He ask this question? Jesus has just taught about the end times.

He points out that in the last days people will be busy with life. They are too busy with life to turn to God in faith. Jesus then teaches the parable of the persistent widow to emphasize the importance of praying and not giving up praying. I think Jesus is communicating a correlation between persistent prayer and faith. How will we know if a Christian community is a people of faith? It is evidenced by their persistence in prayer. But we say, "Life is so full, we don't have time to pray." I am suggesting that when someone is in great need and you are desperate, having gone to the cupboards and found them empty, then you need to seek the resources of our Heavenly Father through a prayer effort. Many have found the prayer efforts listed in this book to be very helpful in aiding them to pray for a crisis or when people are captured by a Kingdom vision in a very focused way for a set period of time. They are amazed at the way the Lord meets with them through their prayer effort. They marvel at the supernatural acts of God that come through these various prayer efforts. Lives are changed when we pray persistently; both the lives of those in need and those who pray.

Through the years the Lord has led my Biblical community and me into ten different prayer efforts:

1. **Daniel Prayer Effort** – A daily prayer effort, seeking the Lord's guidance for a period of twenty-one days.

2. **Prayerful Disciple Making** – A regular practice of prayer where a believer prays persistently for three persons of peace and their households that they may become followers of Christ.

3. **Jericho Prayer Effort** – A gathering of two or more believers to pray for one hour a day for seven days.

4. **On-site Geographical Prayer** – Praying at the location of a strategic Christian gathering to prepare it for the Spirit's anointing.

5. **Overseas Jericho Prayer Effort** – A partnership of a group of believers in the US with a missionary overseas to support a

strategic training or planning event in prayer for a one week period.

6. **Prayer Partners** – Friends, coworkers and gifted intercessors who covenant to pray for a pastor, missionary or Christian leader on a regular basis.

7. **Prayer Walk** – Walking throughout a neighborhood one hour a week, asking God's blessing upon the neighborhood.

8. **Twenty-four Hour Fast** – An act of humility expressed by abstaining from food for twenty-four hours to seek more of God's guidance and power.

9. **Twenty-four Hour Silent Retreat** — A time to withdraw from the busyness of life in order to pursue intimacy with the Father and Son, and hear God's voice, in order to have a sense of God's direction, priority and guidance in life and ministry/work.

10. **Wilderness Prayer Effort** – A gathering of two or more believers participating in a twenty-four hour fast and praying together for one hour on the day of the fast once a week for a period of forty days.

We have watched God show His goodness and justice as we call on Him persistently through these prayer efforts. My hope is that when someone in your life comes to you in great need and you recognize your cupboards are bare, you will respond:

- In compassion and break away from the routine of life,
- In faith and seek the resources of your Heavenly Father, and
- In persistent prayer and participate in one or more of these prayer efforts.

In so doing you will:

- Watch the supernatural hand of your good and just Father in heaven meet the need,

- Experience a fellowship in the Spirit with other members of the Body of Christ through prayer, and
- Be transformed by an encounter with the living Lord Jesus.

Prayer Efforts

DANIEL PRAYER EFFORT

What is a Daniel Prayer Effort?

A Daniel Prayer Effort is a spiritual discipline of prayer where a believer seeks God's direction over a twenty-one day period. It is modeled after Daniel of the Old Testament. Daniel received a vision from the Lord. When he could not interpret the vision, Daniel humbled himself before the Lord and sought His guidance through a partial fast. Daniel fasted for twenty-one days until he received a visitation from an angel. The angel was sent from God the day Daniel began the fast, but a demonic angel, the prince of Persia prohibited the angel from coming to Daniel. Michael, a chief angel came to the angelic messenger's aid and twenty-one days later, through the faithful intercession of Daniel, the visitation came and the interpretation was given. A Daniel Prayer Effort is:

- A persistent seeking of the presence of God. (Jer. 29:12-14)
- A persistent listening to the Holy Spirit for: (John 16:13-15)
    1. Guidance into all truth,
    2. What is yet to come, and
    3. What belongs to Jesus.

How does a Daniel Prayer Effort work?

When a believer is faced with a major decision or is in need of insight from God into a very difficult situation, he is ready for a Daniel Prayer Effort. The believer humbles himself before God through a partial fast of no sugar and meats in his diet. While journaling the believer expresses his:

1. Feelings about the situation he is facing,
2. Desire to meet with the Lord and know His presence,
3. Desire to lay down his plans and agenda, and
4. Questions concerning the situation confronting him.

After he journals these thoughts, he listens for the Holy Spirit's direction. He sets his pen down and waits for the Spirit's leading. John Regier, the Director of Biblical Concepts in Counseling in Colorado Springs, suggests that a believer may hear God through:

1. Passages of Scripture,
2. Songs,
3. Word pictures,
4. Insightful thoughts, and
5. New questions.

Over the course of the twenty-one day period the questions may change. New insight might be given into what Jesus is doing. The Lord may deal with several spiritual formation issues within the believer's life. It will be important to make sure all insight given is:

1. Aligned with Scripture,
2. Confirmed by spouse and family members, and
3. Confirmed by mature mentors.

What would merit a Daniel Prayer Effort?

- Change of career,
- Call to ministry,
- Engagement of marriage,
- Special needs in the life of a son or daughter,
- Job transfer,
- Relocation of family.

PRAYERFUL DISCIPLE MAKING

What is Prayerful Disciple Making?

Prayerful Disciple Making comes out of the teaching of Jesus in Luke 10 as He sent 72 of His followers ahead of Him to preach the gospel of the kingdom. This fivefold plan is being used in the Neighborhood Houses of Prayer Movement in India and the Lighthouses of Prayer Movement in Argentina to mobilize believers to pray for the lost in their lives. In this plan workers in the Lord's harvest field pray for at least three Persons of Peace and their household, with their own household and Biblical community. Persons of Peace are lost people who are responsive, open, and welcoming when a worker in the harvest tells his story or talks about Jesus. The fivefold plan is:

1. **Pray for laborers** - Ask the Father to bring workers into the lives of your Persons of Peace and their households. Ask that your persons of peace will become workers in the harvest to reach their community for Christ.

    And He was saying to them, "The harvest is plentiful, but the laborers are few; therefore beseech the Lord of the harvest to send out laborers into His harvest. Lk 10:2

2. **Pray for God's peace and blessing** - Pray for your three Persons of Peace and their households, persistently asking the Father to bless them and bring peace to their households.

    "Whatever house you enter, first say, 'Peace be to this house.' Lk 10:5

3. **Associate with them** - Associate with your Persons of Peace and their households through coffee, a meal together or participating in an event together and begin investing your life in theirs.

    "Stay in that house, eating and drinking what they give you; for the laborer is worthy of his wages. Do not keep moving from house to house. Lk 10:7

4. **Pray for miracles** - Ask your Persons of Peace how you can pray for them and then pray persistently for the Spirit's power to work miracles in their lives both personally, with your household and corporately with your Biblical community.

   "and heal those in it who are sick," Lk 10:9

5. **Share the gospel** - As your Persons of Peace experience God's blessing, presence and power in their lives, continue to make noise for Jesus and ask if they would be willing to do a Discovery Bible Study with you. Ask the Spirit to open their eyes to a knowledge of who God is and an understanding of the good news of the Kingdom of God.

   "say to them, 'The kingdom of God has come near to you." Lk 10:9

How does the Fivefold Plan for Prayerful Disciple Making work?

1. Pray together with your household and ask the Father to show you three Persons of Peace and their household He wants you to focus your prayer and life on. This could be family, friends, neighbors, your kid's friends or teachers at school, associates, clients, vendors at work, family members, families at the gym or athletic field, etc. List the three persons of peace below:

   _____

   _____

   _____

2. Prepare the ground by praying forty days for your five Persons of Peace and their households, using the Fivefold Plan for Prayerful Disciple Making pray:

   a. *LABORERS*

   Pray that Jesus would send others into the lives of your Persons of Peace and their households and that they themselves will become workers in the harvest to reach their community for Christ. Lk 10:2

b. *PEACE*

Pray that God's blessing & peace would come into the lives of your Persons of Peace and their households. Lk 10:5

c. *ASSOCIATION*

Pray that Jesus will give you wisdom and understanding to know what to do and how to do it as you seek to associate with your Persons of Peace and their households Lk 10:7

d. *MIRACLES*

Pray that the Father will work in miraculous ways to meet the felt needs in the lives of your Persons of Peace and their households to show Himself to be the one true God. Lk 10:9

e. *GOSPEL*

Pray that Jesus will open a door for you to make noise for Him, share your story and lead a Discovery Bible Study with your Persons of Peace. Pray the Spirit will testify of Jesus as you testify of Jesus and convict them of sin, righteousness and judgement. Lk 10:9

3. After you have prayed for your Persons of Peace for forty days, approach them and tell them that you are a part of a Biblical community that is praying for the neighborhood, or school or workplace, or community, etc. Then ask them:

   a. How can we pray for the neighborhood/school/workplace/community?

   b. How can we pray for your family?

   c. How can we pray for you?

4. If they are responsive and give prayer requests, persistently ask the Father to act in miraculous ways in answer their prayer re-

quests, and continue to pray for them using the Fivefold Plan for Prayerful Disciple Making. If they are not responsive, it may be that they are not a Persons of Peace, ask the Lord if He wants you to shake the dust off your feet, move on and begin praying for others.

As the Lord leads, associate with your Persons of Peace, tell them you are praying for them and ask if they have seen God answer their prayer requests. Continue to make noise for Jesus and ask them to join you in a Discovery Bible Study. Invite your Biblical community to join you in reaching out to your Persons of Peace and their households. As you pray, ask the Father to work in a miraculous way in their lives and to bring the reality of the Kingdom of God to them. When they are ready tell them God's story and invite them to trust in Jesus. Begin praying that as your Persons of Peace do Discovery Bible Studies God will open a door for them to lead a Discovery Bible Study with their households.

JERICHO PRAYER EFFORT

What is a Jericho Prayer Effort?

Jericho Prayer is a concept that comes from the Yoido Full Gospel Church in Seoul Korea. In her book, <u>Growing The World's Largest Church</u>,[1] Karen Hurston describes a prayer discipline that God is using to change lives called, "Jericho Prayer." A Jericho Prayer effort is a spiritual discipline of prayer whereby men and women are moved with compassion for someone in need. They break away from the routine of life and seek the goodness and justice of God persistently in prayer for seven days. Joshua and the Children of Israel marched around the city of Jericho for seven days and the Lord delivered the city into their hands. In the same way, believers pray persistently together for seven days for a friend in need and wait for God to show His goodness and justice towards him. A Jericho Prayer effort is a:

1. Persistent pursuit of the goodness of the Father on behalf of a friend who is in need through asking, seeking & knocking, (Luke 11:5-13)
2. Persistent pursuit of the justice of God on behalf of a friend who is in need, (Luke 18:1-8)
3. Corporate prayer gatherings where two or more believers come together in the name of the Lord and agree in prayer, (Matt. 18:18-20) and
4. Spiritual warfare on behalf of a friend who is in bondage. (2 Cor. 10:3-5)

How does a Jericho Prayer work?

When a group of believers are led of the Spirit to pray for one who is in need, they will choose a time to meet on a regular basis to pray for one hour a day for a seven day period. It is preferable to pray in the home of the one in need. Jericho Prayer is a very spontaneous time of prayer where the gathering of believers listens for the Father's voice and prays as the Holy Spirit leads them. Participants are usually surprised by the freshness of each day and the insight given by the Spirit to bring a breakthrough. The following guidelines are very helpful in leading the intercessors into the presence and power of God:

Guidelines for Jericho Prayer:

1. **Praying In Jesus' Name:** When we pray in Jesus' name, we remind ourselves of the source of authority for answered prayer.
2. **Agreeing Prayer:** We recognize that as we agree with one another in prayer, we have promises from Jesus that He will act in a powerful way in answer to our requests.
3. **Spirit Led:** As we pray, we listen for the Holy Spirit's prompting. If a song comes to mind, sing it. If a verse of Scripture comes to mind, quote it or read it out loud.

4. **Praying In One Accord:** We focus our prayers on one request at a time, allowing other members of the group to pray for the same request as they are led. We then move on to another request as the Spirit leads.

5. **Worship:** We enter His gates with thanksgiving and His courts with praise, magnifying the Lord before we begin to make requests of Him. The exhortation of the Psalmist is to enter into the presence of the Lord with an attitude of worship.

What need would merit a Jericho Prayer?

Any time you are moved with compassion for a friend, neighbor, brother or sister in Christ who has a need he/she cannot meet, fix or overcome and you have the faith that God wishes to intervene in a supernatural way; it is time to enter into a Jericho Prayer. Specifically, it could be the salvation of an unbeliever, a financial need, an illness, an addiction or fleshly sin, inner healing, spiritual bondage, a broken marriage, restoration of a brother, reconciliation between two brothers, etc.

ON-SITE GEOGRAPHICAL PRAYER

What is On-site Geographical Prayer?

In his book, Prayer: Key To Revival, Paul Cho makes an insightful statement. "When I preach in Korea or the United States, I pray for two hours. When I preach in Japan or Europe, I pray for three to five hours." He explains that there is a need for a greater duration of prayer when there is greater resistance from the enemy. His experience tells him that there is a greater darkness in some areas than in others. There is a need for a greater work of prayer to break through the darkness and bring in the light of the truth. Through the years I have participated in several On-site Prayer Efforts. Whether it was for a worship service, the national annual meetings for an association of churches, evangelistic meetings or a training seminar, I have experienced and received testimony of a greater freedom to preach, a unity of the Body of Christ and an openness of hearts to the Lord when there has been an on-site prayer effort. On-site Geographical Prayer focuses on:

1. Coming to a place of abiding in order to have a position of authority for intercession, (John 15:7)
2. Listening for the leading of the Holy Spirit, (John 16:12-14)
3. Asserting the work of Christ on the cross and the authority of Jesus in confronting demonic strongholds, (2 Cor 10:3-5; Eph 1:18-22)
4. Interceding for the ministry of the Holy Spirit to reveal Jesus and the truth, (John 14:26; 15:26; 1 Cor 2:10-14) and
5. Laying hands on the leaders of the event and praying for God's anointing to rest upon them. (Luke 4:18,19)

How Does An On-site Geographical Prayer Work?

The individual or a group of believers gather to pray before the event begins. They ask the Holy Spirit how long they will need to pray to bring the breakthrough for an outpouring of the Holy Spirit. The on-site prayer is divided into two parts. In the first part the intercessors approach the throne of grace through worship, Scripture reading and aggressive doctrinal prayer:

1. Affirming the person and work of Christ, and
2. Appropriating the spiritual blessings that are theirs in Christ.

In the second part, the intercessors move throughout the meeting place, listening for the leading of the Holy Spirit and praying at the geographical location where the leaders and participants of the event will be. They stand or kneel at the location and intercede for the:

1. Speaker,
2. Worship leader and team,
3. The one making announcements,
4. The one praying for the offering,
5. Soloists, and

6. Ushers.

Then, starting from the front of the auditorium and moving towards the rear, the intercessors will pray for each row of seats or pews. Finally, the intercessors will approach those who are leading and ask if they can pray for them. Laying hands on the leaders, they ask for the anointing of the Spirit to rest upon them.

OVERSEAS JERICHO PRAYER TEAM

What is an Overseas Jericho Prayer Team?

An Overseas Jericho Prayer Effort is a partnership of a group of believers in the US with a missionary overseas to support a strategic training or planning event in prayer for a one week period. Ideally, seven households (couples and/or singles) would make up an Overseas Jericho Prayer Team. While the missionary is in another nation, the Overseas Jericho Prayer Team is:

1. Pursuing the goodness of the Father through persistent asking, seeking & knocking, (Luke 11:5-13)
2. Pursuing the justice of God to take ground away from the enemy, (Luke 18:1-8)
3. Calling on the intervention of God through fasting, (II Chronicles 20:3)
4. Gathering corporately in the name of the Lord for agreeing prayer, (Matt. 18:18-20) and
5. Engaging in spiritual warfare on behalf of Christian nationals who are in bondage. (2 Cor. 10:3-5)

How does Overseas Jericho Prayer work?

Each team member commits to:

1. Attend at least three prayer gatherings during the week, and
2. Participate in either a food or media fast one of the seven days through the week.

In this way, the prayer team members can still participate, even when schedules are full and there are other commitments through the week. There will be both a prayer gathering and an individual fasting each of the seven days of the week for the ministry event overseas. Each Overseas Jericho Prayer Team member would commit to participate in two Overseas Jericho Prayer Efforts a year for a two year period.

The missionary commits to:

1. Send an email to the Overseas Jericho Prayer Team prior to the trip previewing the ministry event,
2. Send email updates as often as possible through the trip (the goal being daily),
3. Send an email with a summary of all that the Lord did through the trip when he returns, and
4. Meet with the Overseas Jericho Prayer Team, as a group, at least once a year.

Overseas Jericho Prayer Team Roles:

Host – Open his/her home for a daily prayer gathering through the seven day period.

Leader – Lead and coordinate the Jericho Prayer Effort:

1. Inform Overseas Jericho Prayer Team members of the dates, place and time of the prayer effort,
2. Work with the Overseas Jericho Prayer Team members to schedule their participation in both prayer and fasting, and
3. Lead the prayer gatherings.

Email Point Person – Receive the daily prayer updates:

1. Forward the updates to the prayer team, and
2. Make copies and distribute them at the prayer gatherings.

PRAYER PARTNERS

What are Prayer Partners?

Prayer Partners are friends and gifted intercessors who feel led of the Lord to pray regularly for a pastor, missionary or Christian leader. After a number of nationally known Christian evangelists fell during the 80's, Peter Wagner and John Maxwell began teaching on the importance of Prayer Partners. Peter says that "Prayer Partners are the most underutilized source of God's power in the church today."[1]

Where does this concept of prayer partners come from in Scripture? It comes from Exodus 17 where Moses gives a picture of the power of a praying leader and the necessity of praying partners to sustain him. On this occasion, the Amalekites came out to fight against the nation of Israel in the wilderness. There are two battle stations within this conflict:

1. Joshua and the Israel army are in the valley engaging the enemy in physical combat, and

2. Moses, with Aaron and Ur, is on the hill engaging in spiritual warfare in a different way. Moses' hands are lifted with the staff of God in them.

The key to the victory that day was the warfare taking place on the hill. As Moses raised the staff of God, the Children of Israel prevailed in the battle. When the staff was lowered, the Amalekites prevailed. For Joshua and the children of Israel, the staff of God represented the power of God. It was as Moses lifted the staff of God over the Red Sea, God parted the Sea and the Children of Israel walked across it on dry ground. When Moses lifted the staff a second time, God closed the Red Sea on Pharaoh and his army and they drowned. There was a necessity for support in the battle with the Amalekites if the victory was to be secured. After a period of time, Moses' hands grew heavy and were lowered from fatigue. Moses didn't have the strength to keep his hands up throughout the day. Aaron and Hur were with Moses on the hill and saw the relationship between the raised staff in Moses' hands and the victory in the valley below. So they held up Moses' hands with the staff of God and the battle was won in the valley.

In the same manner as Aaron and Hur supported Moses in his warfare, so the primary purpose of Prayer Partners is to pray for the Christian leader so that the leader can pray for his ministry. No one can pray the prayers of the Christian leader. There is a unique anointing and authority the Lord has given to the leader that only he can assert in prayer and bring victory in his ministry. Prayer Partners focus their prayers for:

1. Protection from the evil one for the leader and his family, as well as a sanctified life for them, (John 17:9-19)

2. Presence of the Lord Jesus to be revealed to the leader, (Eph. 1:17-19; 3:16-19)

3. Guidance of the Holy Spirit to give wisdom and understanding into the will of the Lord for the leader, (Col. 1:9-12) and

4. Opening of doors of ministry and giving boldness to the leader to fulfill God's calling in his life. (Col. 4:2-4; Eph. 6:19)

How does Prayer Partners work?

It always works best if the Christian leader and the Prayer Partner have a relationship of prayer. The Christian leader commits to communicating both answers to prayer and prayer requests at least monthly. The Prayer Partner commits to pray for the Christian leader regularly. This can be once a week, daily or daily with an added special focus one day a week. It would behoove the Christian leader to communicate more frequently with a Prayer Partner who is a gifted intercessor and more watchful in their prayers.

Many Christian leaders have stepped away from Prayer Partners because the Prayer Partner has broken the bond of trust with the leader. Several guidelines essential to Prayer Partners are:

1. *Confidentiality* – what is shared with the Prayer Partner stays with the Prayer Partner,

2. *Servanthood* – the Prayer Partner has an assignment to pray for the Christian leader and has no other expectations of the leader, and

1. *Non-judgmental* – the Prayer Partner does not have a role to correct or reprove the Christian leader. Rather it is a role of prayer and prayer alone, unless there is an indication of immorality, unethical practices or heresy which need to be confronted. The Prayer Partner needs to pray that the Christian leader will surround himself with mentors who will hold him accountable.

Who needs Prayer Partners?

Any Christian leader who is advancing the Kingdom of God and therefore is a target of the enemy.

PRAYER WALKS

What is a Prayer Walk?

Prayer walking is a movement of the Spirit throughout the United States where believers are asking for God's blessing on their neighborhoods. A Prayer Walk is a spiritual discipline of prayer whereby men and women are so moved with compassion for the lost and filled with faith that they break away from the routine of life and prayerfully walk through their neighborhoods. In so doing, the Spirit of God begins to usher the reality of the presence and power of Jesus in their neighborhoods. The Kingdom of God will be near!

A Prayer Walk is:

1. Calling on the goodness of God to show His favor on your neighborhood by blessing the households you pass and asking for God's peace within those homes as you walk, (Luke 4:16-19; 10:5,6)

2. Claiming your neighborhood for Jesus Christ by affirming God's sovereign call in your life and affirming that He is placing households in your hand, (John 3:27,28,34,35; 17:2-4,18)

3. Spiritual warfare whereby we declare the truth and serve notice to the powers of darkness that Jesus is building His church and their gates cannot prevail against it, (Matt 11:12; 16:18,19: 2 Cor. 10:4,5) and

4. Asking God to make the presence of the Lord Jesus real to every household within your neighborhood by the Spirit. (Luke 10:21,22; John 15:26,27; 1 Cor. 2:9,10)

How does a Prayer Walk work?

A Prayer Walk begins when a believer realizes that God wishes to show His favor to his neighborhood and senses God's call to pray for the households of his neighborhood. The believer sets aside at least one hour weekly to walk the streets of his neighborhood. A Prayer Walk is a Spirit led time of prayer, where the believer is worshipping God and listening for His voice. He listens for the needs God wishes to touch within his neighborhood. He listens for promises from God's word to claim on their behalf.

As he walks, he first prays for God's blessing and peace to fall on the households within his neighborhood. Second, he affirms God's call in his life and the lost souls God is giving to him. Third, he serves notice to the powers of darkness by the authority of the exalted Jesus and by faith declares what Jesus is doing in his neighborhood. Finally, he asks the Father for the ministry of the Spirit to reveal the presence of Jesus in each household within his neighborhood.

It is important that the prayer walker secure the commitment from his Biblical community and gifted intercessors to pray daily for the Spirit's leading and protection for him and his family from the spiritual attacks of the enemy.

TWENTY-FOUR HOUR FAST

What does it mean to fast?

To fast is to abstain from food for a spiritual purpose to either draw near to God for greater intimacy and worship or to seek more of His intervention for guidance, power and/or protection to do His will. Fasting is an act of humility. It is saying to God, "I need you more than I need food!" And God gives grace to the humble. It is saying, "God, I need more...more of you. I want to give you more of my praise and worship. I need more of your guidance...more of your power...more of your protection...more of Your grace and compassion." The very nature of a fast is a grieving or mourning over a situation that only God can change.

Why did Biblical leaders fast?

- **Moses** received more of God and His instruction. (Exodus 34:28)
- **Israel** needed more of God's deliverance. (I Samuel 7:6)
- **Jehoshaphat** needed more of God's wisdom & intervention. (II Chronicles 20:3)
- The **King of Nineveh** needed more of God's compassion & grace. (Jonah 3:5,6)
- **Daniel** needed more of God's understanding. (Daniel 10:1-3)
- **Ezra** needed more of God's protection. (Ezra 8:21-23)
- **Nehemiah** needed more of God's wisdom & intervention. (Nehemiah 1:4)
- **Esther** needed more of God's intervention. (Esther 4:15-17)
- **Anna** wanted to give more worship to God. (Luke 2:37)
- **Jesus** needed more of God's strength. (Matt. 4:1-11)
- **Prophets and teachers** wanted to give God greater worship. (Acts 13:1-3)

- **Paul and Barnabas** needed God's anointing for themselves and others. (Acts 13:1-3; 14:23)

How do we fast for twenty-four hours?

We enter a fast as led by the Spirit of God. It is a heart response of wanting more of God. It is not to be entered into for show or personal ambition. It is built upon a life that is already yielded to God. And if our life is not yet yielded, that would be the very purpose of the fast.

During a twenty-four hour fast:

1. Allow yourself to be led and stirred with a sense of need by the Spirit of God.
2. Determine to not eat food after eating one meal (i.e. dinner, lunch or breakfast) until you sit down to eat the same meal the next day.
3. Devote the normal time allotted to the two meals missed, as well as your normal quiet time to meditate, to pray and study concerning the focus of your fast.
4. As you feel discomfort in the last few hours of your fast, use the discomfort to remind you of your need for God and utter breath prayers concerning your focus. (A breath prayer is a simple address to one of the members of the Godhead followed by a simple request, i.e. "Father, set him free!")[1]
5. Practice this discipline weekly until you are released by the Spirit of God to stop.

You might want to consider fasting if:

- You are struggling in a conflict with a brother or sister in Christ.
- You need direction for your life.
- You need freedom from bondage.
- God seems far off.

- Someone within your family is ill.
- You want to give more of yourself to God.
- You don't feel safe in your home or community.
- There are people going hungry or without shelter in your community.
- There is prejudice within your community.
- Your children are rebellious or cold towards God.
- You and your spouse cannot reconcile your differences.
- You want to see the lost come to Christ.
- You are indifferent to the eternal destiny of the lost.

TWENTY-FOUR HOUR SILENT RETREAT

Purpose:

The purpose of this silent retreat is to withdraw from the busyness of life in order to pursue intimacy with the Father and Son and hear God's voice, so that I may have a sense of God's direction, priority and guidance in my life and ministry.

Materials needed:

- Bible
- Computer or electronic device with Bible App.
- Journal
- A Spiritual Reading (a devotional book focusing on prayer and contemplation or a biography)
- Pencil or Pen

I. Reflecting on the past month/quarter/year: (after lunch and through the early after noon)

It is time to enter into a period of silence for twenty-four hours. Ask the Spirit to help you to enter into this spiritual discipline of silence and to give you grace to fulfill it. Silence means silence. You commit to not speak or sing aloud even with yourself, let alone with another. Abstain from listening to the radio, TV, internet, smart phone, etc. You are listening to your heart for that is where God converses with His children.

Ask the Holy Spirit, the Helper, to guide you through the next day of silence and reflection. Give Him permission to change your agenda and to reveal to you what Jesus is doing in your life and ministry/business. This time of quiet reflection is a pursuit of the presence of God and not a pursuit of a plan. Step away from your need to fix and problem-solve, and sit at the feet of Jesus or enter into the arms of your Heavenly Father. It is as you enter into and experience the presence of the Father and/or Son that you will hear His purpose, priority and plan for your life and ministry/business.

Reflect on the past month/quarter/year and write a letter to the Father/Son about all that you felt through that period of time. Hone in on what you are feeling, why you are feeling that way and what it prompts you to do. Emotions are a window into the soul. They reveal what is going on in your heart. Ask the Holy Spirit to reveal your heart, for out of your heart, flows the springs of life (Proverbs 4:23).

What comes to mind first? Write a letter to your Heavenly Father or the Son about everything in your journal. (Depending on your outlook on life, whether you see the glass half full or half empty, you will immediately focus on the positive or the negative. It doesn't matter which comes first.) Talk to God about the experiences and emotions that are on the surface as you write. Be honest with the Father as you celebrate and/or grieve. Honesty is the key. Respond to the Father/Son. Your response may be filled with thanksgiving and praise. It may be filled with sorrow and a sacrifice of thanksgiving. Ask the Spirit to help you in your response.

Spend the first part of the afternoon with this kind of reflection in the presence of the Father and/or Son. Go for walks. Give yourself the freedom to take a nap. This is a time to cease striving and enter into the presence of God. It takes time to enter into the presence of the Living God.

II. Listening for God's truth for you: (late afternoon)

Ask the Spirit of truth to guide you into all truth. Seek the face of the Living God. Reflect on the emotions you felt this afternoon and write about them in your journal. What was the predominate emotions you felt? Why did you feel them? What do they prompt you to do? Your emotions give you a peak into the condition of your heart. Discern the source of the voices you heard. Were they from the Father/Son or were they from your own ambition or were they from the enemy? Now put your pen down and listen for the voice of the Father/Son to you. Ask the Helper to reveal the Father/Son to you. You may want to go for a walk and quietly listen. You may want to be still within your chair and quietly listen. Now indent from the margin you have been using and write in your journal what you hear in your heart. You will hear a verse of Scripture, a song, a word picture, a spontaneous thought and/or a new question. What is the Father/Son saying to you?

(If you don't hear anything, you may want to ask the Father/Son who you need to forgive. Often, when God is silent there is bitterness in our heart. Forgive that person(s) and release him/them to God. You may have a proud heart. God is opposed to the proud. Repent and humble yourself before the Father/Son. Ask the Spirit to help you in these things that you may get right with God and hear His voice.)

Openness and honesty is so important here. Take off the masks and be real with God. He wants to speak to your heart. The Father/Son wants to speak truth to you, comforting you, affirming you. Allow yourself to have an encounter with the living God. After a time of receiving and enjoying the presence of God, ask Him to reveal His agenda for your time with Him tonight. What does He want you to focus on? What does He want you to grow in? Again, you will hear a verse of Scripture, a song, a word picture, a spontaneous thought and/or a new question. Ask Him to instruct your heart. Jesus said, "Come to Me all who are weary and heavy-laden, and I will give you rest. Take My yoke upon you and learn from Me, for I am gentle and humble in heart, and you will find rest for your souls. For My yoke is easy and My burden is light," (Matt. 11:28). Tell Him how you want to learn from Him.

DINNER

III. Learning from Jesus: (evening)

Pursue the presence of the Father/Son. Write a love letter to Him in your journal. Ask the Spirit to be your Helper through the day. Ask the Spirit to guide you into all truth. You may be searching the truth of Scripture to confront the lies and negative emotions of the enemy through a word study. You may be digging deeper into the Word of God to know His promises to you to bring healing to your wounded heart through devotional reading of Scripture. You may be plumbing the depths of the Word of Truth to know the character of Your God through meditation upon a passage of Scripture. You may be sitting at the feet of a historical or contemporary mentor, as you read the Spiritual Reading the Spirit led you to bring. In all of this, take a posture of a learner before the Father/Son. Receive the things you read as the very words of God to you! Throughout the night respond to the Father/Son and tell Him what you are learning. Let Him speak to your heart.

BREAKFAST

IV. Pursuing God's Direction: (late night or early morning)

In your journal, write out a description of the Lord's calling in your life and ministry. List the promises He has given you. Prayerfully affirm your calling in ministry from the Lord Jesus. Ask the Lord Jesus to show you what He wants to do in your life and your ministry in the next month/quarter/year. What is Jesus doing in your life? What is Jesus doing in your family? What is Jesus doing in the lives of those (employees, clients, vendors, staff, congregation, community, industry, etc.) He has entrusted to you? What does the Lord want you to do in each case? Begin knocking on a door, asking the Lord Jesus to bring to pass what he is directing you to do.

V. Seeking God's Promises and Priority: (late morning)

Continue knocking on a door, asking Jesus to transform your life and your ministry/business in the coming month/quarter/year.

Ask the Lord to give you a promise from His word that will sustain you as you pursue the things He is directing you to do.

Ask Him to give you a sense of priority for say yes to and what He wants you to say no to.

Ask the Spirit to give you wisdom and understanding to know what to do and how to do it in the coming weeks, as you seek to obey His will. Recognize the difference between goals and desires.

Goals are things you have control over, so ask the Spirit what are the goals He wants you to set, and then assume responsibility for them. In setting goals, be careful not to become too detailed here. Set one to three broader goals for your coming month/quarter/year. Save the details for your weekly and daily planning.

Desires are things you have no control over (people, places and things), so turn them over to God and knock on a door through the month/quarter/year, asking the Father to intervene and bring to pass the things He is doing.

WILDERNESS PRAYER EFFORT

What is a Wilderness Prayer effort?

Wilderness Prayer combines the principles of three other prayer strategies: Persistent Prayer, a Twenty-four Hour fast and a Jericho Prayer effort over a period of forty days. We discovered this powerful prayer effort in the summer of 1997 when the staff and Saturday morning intercessors of Pantego Bible Church entered into this pattern of prayer for a pastor's wife. We watched God heal her as a result of this work of prayer. This is a forty-day prayer effort where a group of people prays persistently and fasts one day a week. On the day they fast, they will gather to war in prayer for one hour.

A Wilderness Prayer Effort is:

1. A forty-day prayer effort where believers commit themselves to a spiritual warfare of persistent prayer for a six-week period. Forty has the idea of testing in the Scriptures. Somehow in God's economy it is a significant number that brings spiritual breakthroughs, (Exodus 34:28; 1 Kings 19:8,9)

2. A corporate prayer gathering where two or more believers come together in the name of the Lord and agree together in prayer, (Matt. 18:18-20)

3. A persistent pursuit of the goodness of the Father through asking, seeking and knocking on behalf of an acquaintance or group who is in need, (Luke11:5-13)

4. A persistent pursuit of the justice of God on behalf of an acquaintance or group who is in need, (Luke 18:1-8) and

5. A fast one day a week through the six-week period, (Exodus 34:28; Luke 4:1,2)

How does a Wilderness Prayer work?

When a group of people or an individual:

1. Is moved with compassion for an individual or group who is in need,

2. Believe that God is good, just and able to deliver that person through the power of Jesus and His shed blood on the cross, and

3. Sense the leading of the Holy Spirit to join together in prayer, then they are ready to enter into a Wilderness Prayer effort.

Before starting the Wilderness Prayer Effort, they will want to agree on the day and time they will fast for a 24-hour period (dinner to dinner, lunch to lunch or breakfast to breakfast). They will also need to agree on the time and place where they will gather to pray for one-hour. In the 24-four hour fast they will want to:

1. Allow themselves to be stirred with a sense of need and be led by the Spirit of God,

2. Devote the normal time allotted to the two meals missed, as well as their normal quiet time to meditate, pray and study concerning the focus of their Wilderness Prayer Effort, and

3. As they feel discomfort in the last few hours of the fast, use the discomfort to remind them of their need for God and utter breath prayers concerning the focus. (A breath prayer[1] is a simple address to one of the members of the Godhead followed by a simple request, i.e. "Father, set him free!")

Guidelines for the Wilderness Prayer time:

1. **Praying In Jesus' Name:** When we pray in Jesus' name, we remind ourselves of the source of authority for answered prayer.

2. **Agreeing Prayer:** We recognize that as we agree with one another in prayer, we have promises from Jesus that He will act in a powerful way in answer to the request.

3. **Spirit Led:** As we pray, we listen for the Holy Spirit's prompting. If a song comes to mind, sing it. If a verse of Scripture comes to mind, quote it or read it out loud.

4. **Praying In One Accord:** We focus our prayers on one request at a time, allowing other members of the group to pray for the same request as they are led. We then move on to another request as the Spirit leads.

5. **Worship:** We enter His gates with thanksgiving and His courts with praise, magnifying the Lord before we begin to make re-

quests of Him. The exhortation of the Psalmist is to enter into the presence of the Lord with an attitude of worship.

What need would merit a Wilderness Prayer?

After one or more individuals have already prayed (persistent prayer, fasting, Jericho Prayer, etc.) for someone in bondage with no measurable results, they may want to enter into a Wilderness Prayer Effort. There might be demonic bondage present that is characterized by fleshly addictive sins, strongholds of deception, or destruction or oppression brought on by curses or generational sin.

Appendix

ENCOUNTERING GOD TOGETHER,
Five Guidelines to Prayer

How many times have you been part of a small group and the leader says, "Tonight we have an hour for praying and sharing. Are there any prayer requests?" Fifty-five minutes later the leader looks at his watch and says, "My, where has the time gone?" He reminds the group to pray for the requests through the week and then asks one of the group members to close the time in prayer.

Unfortunately this is the experience of many small groups throughout America. In those fifty-five minutes of sharing a good deal of caring has taken place. But the group never tapped into the awesome power of God through prayer. Although they may have a sense of being cared for, they rarely encounter their loving heavenly Father and His power.

Suppose the group never took prayer requests? Consider what would happen if the group reviewed a few guidelines for prayer and then poured out their hearts to their Father for 55 minutes in prayer. The following guidelines to prayer will assist any prayer gathering to pray more effectively and watch God work.

1. Praying in Jesus' Name:

When we pray in Jesus' name, we remind ourselves of the source of authority for answered prayer.

On the night before His death, Jesus promised His disciples six times that whatever they asked in His name, He would do for them.

Until now you have not asked for anything in My name. Ask and you will receive, and your joy will be complete. John 16:24

When Jesus says something once, we should respond to Him. When He says something twice, we need to take note. When He says something six times, do you think He's trying to make a point? There is power when we pray in Jesus' name!

When we pray in Jesus' name we are drawing on the riches of Jesus' account in the heavenly realms. Several years ago my family banked at a small credit union. There were only three ladies working on the floor. They knew each member of my family by name. It is conceivable that if my oldest daughter, Kara, were to approach the clerk's window with a check signed by me that the clerk would recognize Kara and cash the check. However, if Kara signed the check and handed it to the clerk, she would never honor it. The reason being, Kara didn't have an account at the credit union. Even though the clerk recognized Kara and knew that she was my daughter, the clerk would not give her any funds because she had no funds to draw upon. In the same way, when we approach our Heavenly Father in prayer, although the Father knows us as His children and loves us, we don't have an account. It is only as we make our requests known in the name of His Son, Jesus, that the Father then responds by drawing on Jesus' account.

As we approach the Father in prayer we have nothing in our account to draw upon; it is only Jesus who has the resources to supply our needs in answer to our prayers in the heavenly realms. So when we pray, we use the phrase, "In Jesus' name," at the beginning of our request or at the end of our request. "Heavenly Father, in Jesus' name, would you... or Lord God, we want to ask that you would...in Jesus' name." In so doing we are reminding ourselves of the source of answered prayer.

2. Agreeing Prayer:

As we agree with one another in prayer, we have promises from Jesus that He will act in a powerful way in answer to the request.

When instructing His disciples how to pray for someone who had sinned against a brother and refused to repent, Jesus promised that if two of them agreed upon anything together that He would do whatever they asked.

Again, I tell you that if two of you on earth agree about anything you ask for, it will be done for you by My Father in heaven. Matthew 18:19

Somehow within God's economy there is greater power in prayer when we pray with others and agree together on the requests we make. When I was a young Christian, I participated in a Thursday night youth Bible study. We met with our youth pastor, Dave, and his wife in their little home, squeezing 15 to 20 students into their small living space. At the end of the Bible study we would pray for one another's needs. One night as we were praying, I noticed that Dave would softly grunt, "gruuum," during the prayer time. After several weeks I realized that if Dave was grunting for someone's prayer, it meant that he liked it. I always felt very affirmed when Dave would grunt, "gruuum," as I prayed. Years later I realized that Dave was agreeing with us in prayer.

Agreement in prayer allows for everyone in the group to contribute to the prayer effort. There might be members of the group who are new to prayer and feel uncomfortable praying aloud. Even though they do not feel comfortable praying aloud they can still be a part of the prayer time as they agree with the requests that are prayed for. We can agree in prayer silently, but I would suggest that the members of the group consider giving some kind of verbal affirmation as they agree with a prayer request. A verbal expression like, "Amen!" or "Yes Lord!" could do. I like to say, "In Jesus' name!" or even, *"Gruuum!"* In so doing, Jesus has given us a very special promise from His word that He will answer our prayers.

3. Spirit Led:

We listen for the Holy Spirit's prompting. If a song comes to mind, sing it. If a verse of scripture comes to mind, quote it or read it aloud. As the Apostle Paul exhorted the Ephesian believers to put on the armor of God he also instructed them to pray in the Spirit.

And pray in the Spirit on all occasions with all kinds of prayers and requests. With this in mind, be alert and always keep on praying for all the saints. Ephesians 6:18

To pray in the Spirit is to let the Holy Spirit guide us as we pray. Jesus said that He would send another counselor who would guide His disciples into all truth. He said that the Spirit would speak only what He hears and He would tell us what is yet to come. He would bring glory to Jesus by making known to us the things that belong to Christ. How can a group of people pray for an hour? What would they say after each request has been prayed for? What I am suggesting here is that we not pray through a list, but rather, we pray for one another as the Spirit leads. Have you ever prayed within a group and were about to open your mouth with a request and at that very same moment another person prayed the very words you were going to say? It's happened to me, time and time again. I use to think, "that person just stole my prayer!" Then I realized that we were listening to the same Spirit and thought, "Wow, we are both hearing God!"

When a group of ten people come together to pray there are actually eleven persons in the room as they approach the throne of grace. The Spirit of God is there! He indwells every believer and desires to guide each one as they pray. He will give a song or a verse of Scripture to the members of the group. He will bring someone to mind or give insight in how to pray for a situation. A friend once said, "When you receive an impression give it an expression."

Listening for the leading for the Spirit is like listening to background music at a dentist office. Many years ago, as a young adult I was in a dentist office. I knew that the dentist was going to drill out a cavity and fill it. Being anxious about the impending pain I was going to experience, I picked up a magazine and began to thumb through it. As I waited, some soft and soothing FM music was playing and I heard a song that reminded me of a very special time in my teenage years. The song was "Silence Is Golden," a hit song in the late 60's.

As I heard the song, I was no longer in the dentist office; I was in a car with my brothers and friends driving down Pacific Coast Highway. The sky was blue. The waves were breaking on the Malibu coast. The air was crisp. That same song, "Silence Is Golden, Golden..." came over the radio station we were listening to in the car. For a moment, my fears of pain were gone and I was enjoying a warm memory of special times in the past.

Several years later, I woke up early in the morning to pray and a song of praise was on my heart. I thought, "that's neat but I've got to pray!" So I got out of bed, got dressed and began to make some coffee for my prayer walk when I heard the song again. Once again I thought, "That's great, but I've got to pray!" As I began my prayer walk, the song came back again and I thought, "I like that song, but I've got to pray!" Then all of a sudden it hit me that the Spirit was giving me this song. So I gave an expression to the impression the Spirit had given and sang it out. As I sang and praised the Lord, I was ushered into His presence and it became the focus of my prayer walk. It was a powerful time of prayer! Too often we enter into prayer with the burden of the request, kind of like the anticipation of pain in the dentist office. But when we are still and listen for the Sprit's leading, we are ushered into the presence of God. There is a great sense of power in prayer when the group lets the Spirit of God lead their prayer time. The group knows that they are praying the very things that are on the heart of Jesus.

4. Praying in One Accord:

We pray for one request at a time, allowing other members of the group to pray for that same request. We then move on to another request as the Spirit leads.

The Apostle Paul exhorted the Philippian believers to be one in all that they do.

If you have any encouragement from being united with Christ, if any comfort from His love, if any fellowship with the Spirit, if any tenderness and compassion, then make my joy complete by being likeminded, having the same love, being one in spirit and purpose. Philippians 2:1,2

When a small group of believers pray, there is the potential for them to share in an encouragement from being united in Christ, comforted by His love and a fellowship with the Spirit. This notion of praying in one accord is hard for some because it requires submission to one another.

Have you ever had a sense that you were at a horse race as you prayed in a small group of believers? The horses are in the gate. They are ready to go. Then, ding-a-ling-a-ling and they are off! One intercessor prays for one prayer concern, then another, and another and another until every prayer concern has been prayed for. The rest of the members of the group are saying to themselves, "I guess we're all done, everything has been prayed for?" That one lone prayer warrior, no matter how effectual his prayers, has robbed the rest of the group of an opportunity to pray for those needs as well.

Have you ever felt like you were playing hop-scotch when you prayed in a group? Hopscotch is a game all the kids on my street used to play when I was a kid. We would draw 10 squares on a sidewalk. Throw a small object in a square and then hop over the square with the object to the other squares, leaping from one square to the other. Sometimes our group prayer times are just like that. As we begin praying within the group, one member will pray for two or three requests. Then another member of the group will pray for two or three requests, sometimes the same and sometimes different. Then another member of the group will pray for two or three more requests, again, some different, some the same. Although every request is prayed for, the group never enters into a fellowship with the Spirit or with one another in prayer.

When we pray in one accord we choose to pray for one thing at a time. As one person is led by the Spirit to pray for a concern, the other members of the group don't change the topic of concern, but submit to the one praying and piggyback on that person's prayer, praying for the same concern as the Spirit leads. Then after all have prayed who are led and a few seconds of silence has passed, another member of the group leads out in prayer for a different situation or person as the Spirit directs. The other members of the group may piggyback on that prayer, as the Spirit leads, as well. Each prayer for that one concern might be different. It is not that one person's prayer is more insightful or better than another, but that the body of Christ is now at work. Each member of the group prays according to his/her gifts and experience with the result that each concern is bathed in prayer.

The difference between hopscotch prayers and praying in one accord is like the difference between cleaning spit-up off a baby and bathing a baby. When I was a young parent and we spent the day with friends it was natural for my baby daughter to spit-up food through the day. We always had a cloth or a diaper handy to clean off the spit-up. At the end of the day our baby appeared to be clean, but one sniff told another story because our baby's spit-up had soured and begun to smell. On the other hand, when we would bath one of my daughters we took off her smelly clothes, placed her into the bath water and rinsed her. Methodically, we would wash each part of her body and then rinse off the soapy water. Now our baby is clean! In the same way, when we pray in one accord, praying for one thing at a time and piggybacking on one another's prayers, we bathe each concern in prayer.

5. Worship:

We enter His gates with thanksgiving and His courts with praise, magnifying the Lord before we begin to make requests of Him.

The exhortation of the Psalmist is to enter into the presence of the Lord with an attitude of worship.

Enter His gates with thanksgiving and His courts with praise; give thanks to Him and praise His name. Psalm 100:4

Too often, we rush into the presence of God with intercession. We are filled with the burden of the needs we are facing. There are times when this is very appropriate, because the Spirit of God is ushering us into intercession immediately. However, when we rush into intercession too quickly the need seems to be too big and God seems to be too small in our prayer gatherings. I am going to suggest that, as a rule, it is important to focus on the greatness of God before we ever focus on the pressing needs that confront us. As we magnify the Lord Jesus, who is seated at the right hand of the Father and has all authority in heaven and on earth, all of a sudden, everything is put into perspective. God is God! He is able! We are now ready to bring the pressing needs of our lives to Him who is able to do exceedingly abundant beyond all we can ask or think.

As the Spirit leads, enter the presence of the Lord with thanksgiving and praise. If the Spirit gives you a hymn or a song, sing it. If He gives you a Psalm or a doxology, read it aloud. In one accord give thanks and praise God for one thing at a time and then piggy-back on one another's expressions of praise. Take your time. Come to that place of abiding/oneness as members of the body of Christ, seated with Jesus at the right hand of the Father. Now, you are ready to intercede with authority and faith!

When a group prays within the parameters of the five prayer guidelines there is a new sense of power! The group can have confidence that the Father will hear them as they pray in Jesus' name and agree with one another in prayer. The group experiences a new encounter with the Father as they share in a fellowship with the Spirit and yield to one another. When they begin with thanksgiving and praise, there is a sense of God's presence and power that is altogether different than just sharing prayer requests. This powerful encounter with the Father is life changing and glorious.

Notes
Persistent Asking, Seeking & Knocking
1. Paul Y. Cho, *PRAYER: Key to Revival* (Waco, Texas: Word 1984) 49-52
2. Paul Y. Cho, *PRAYER: Key to Revival* (Waco, Texas: Word 1984) 61-63

Jericho Prayer
1. Karen Hurston, *Growing the World's Largest Church* (Springfield, Missouri: Chrism 1994) 47,48

Prayer Partners
1. Peter Wagner, *The Prayer Shield* (Ventura, California: Regal Books 1992) 19

The Twenty-four Hour Fast
1. Richard Foster, *PRAYER, Finding The Hearts True Home*, (San Francisco, California: HarperCollins Publishers 1992) 122-124

Wilderness Prayer
1. Richard Foster, *PRAYER, Finding The Hearts True Home*, (San Francisco, California: HarperCollins Publishers 1992) 122-124

ABOUT THE AUTHOR

Clyde was born and grew up in Southern California. He is a graduate of Biola University and Talbot Theological Seminary. He and his wife, Mary Lynne, were married in June 1976. They have three daughters Kara, Lindsay and Meagan, and are thankful for their growing family through marriage and grandchildren.

Mary Lynne and Clyde's youth pastor, Dave Griener, mentored them to love God's word and hear His voice through the word. Dave taught them to study and memorize God's word, as well as, to pray for hours. Clyde has always been given to prayer because of the grounding he received in those early days of faith in Christ. An intercessory gift began to emerge in 1984, as Clyde experienced frustration with the lack of fruitfulness in ministry. Prayer became a part of everything he did. Clyde has watched the Father fulfill His promises to answer prayer over and over again. Clyde has been equipping the Body of Christ to pray and has led a variety of prayer efforts since 1989.

Clyde served in various associate pastoral positions for twenty-five years and sensed God's call to pray for the nations in November of 2000. He was the Director of Prayer Ministries at MentorLink International through 2008 and then launched PrayerMentor ministry, where he serves as the President. Through these ministries he's led prayer efforts and equipped christian leaders in 25 nations through 55 international trips.

Clyde mentors pastors, ministry leaders and business owners in prayer, cares for their souls and builds prayer teams around them so that they may fulfill the work Jesus has given to them, thereby glorifying the Father and advancing the Kingdom of God on earth. In 2011, Clyde and Mary Lynne began intentionally discipling international students and praying in the villages of unreached people groups to bring about Disciple Making Movements among the nations.

A Prayer Mentor Booklet Series

Coming to a Place of Abiding

Equipping believers to come to a place of abiding by appropriating the present ministry of Jesus in the heavenly realms through the Yahweh prayers.

God's Calling

Equipping Christian leaders and intercessors to discern God's calling in their lives and assert the authority of their calling as forceful men and women by praying Kingdom prayers through the themes of John.

Persistent Prayer

Equipping the body of Christ to persist in prayer through a variety of prayer efforts in order to fulfill the calling of the Lord Jesus in their lives.

Made in the USA
Middletown, DE
17 September 2018